AUSTRALIANA
Poems

Ocean to the Outback

JENNY MAC

JENNY MAC

Copyright © 2021 Jenny Mac
All rights reserved.

ISBN 978 0 6483536 4 5 (Paperback)

No part of this publication may be reproduced or transmitted in any form or by any means, without permission in writing from The Author.

POEMS

Australian Author: Jenny Mac

The Author JENNY MAC was born in the Country of Central Australia, but now lives near the ocean on the Central Coast of NSW in Australia, where she completed the sequel 'CHEYLA' to her first Novel 'April Rain.' from The Australian Outback Series.
Website   www.jennymac.com.au

Other Titles by Author: Jenny Mac

Fiction Novels:
'The Australian Outback Series'
'APRIL RAIN' Book 1
'CHEYLA' Highway of Infinity Book 2

JENNY MAC

Australian Birdlife

Galah

Rainbow Lorikeet

White Cockatoo

Black Cockatoo

Major Mitchell

POEMS

Australiana
Poems
'Ocean to the Outback'

Kookaburra

What better way to portray Australia than with Australian Birdlife
In tree-tops or flying high distinctive bird-life fill Australia's sky
So many specific Australian species stand-outs to say the least
'Australian Birdlife' is a-plenty all striving for food on the fly
On a hunt to eat is their life's work to feed nested young nearby
Such an opportune time is to visit a natural habitat when they feast

Just to hear a Kookaburra laugh is no myth Australians say
So unique is its call from the gum trees way up high
Beautiful lorikeets seek nectar from native floral blooms at bay
Cockatoos Galahs or parrots galore just to name a few are nigh
True Australians born and bred in flight to give pleasure each day.

White Cockatoo, Lorikeet, Galah

JENNY MAC

Australia

POEMS

Australia's Pride

This is our land Australia so primitive yet so diverse
Passed on from our forefather's and their sweat in mother earth
It is our home we cherish it but strive to protect it first
As so many have lost their lives just to prove our Country's worth

We share its vastness its beauty and so many treasures to behold
In this our sunburnt country that we grew up in and love
Though tales around a campfire say the land gives back threefold
Some beg to differ though stories prove it is a treasure from above

Yes this is Australia where the wattle trees proudly grow
The unmistakable yellow blooms spreading colour across the land
Amidst fauna tall gum-trees stand proud with other species in tow
Weeping Willows bow down to rivers with roots set deep in sand

Out in paddocks cattle graze sheep strive to share the acres
Of produce meat and wool assuring Australia to be rich in trading
With endless demands satisfied and rewards go to their makers
Other crops of wheat, rice, sugar cane grown are in the making

Though deep in the earth rich in minerals precious gems are sort
Our land simply amassed with a variety of riches to be found
Of Iron-ore coal and gold… Who would have thought
Only huge machinery could free it from the ground
Australia a land we live in…To be Australian is 'Australia's pride.'

JENNY MAC

Whispers in the Wind: ACT

POEMS

Australian Capital Territory

Whispers in the Wind

It was in The Nation's Capital that word was passed around
Severe drought now evident came calls from sources deep within
Land drying up from lack of rain and no grasses to be found
'Aussie Farmers doing it tough' were the 'Whispers in the Wind'

It was a major disaster so no crops could be sown
Working daylight to dusk with no results they could not bare
If this kept up no doubt their budget would be blown
There was urgent need of rain but no water to be spared
Out in the paddocks sheep and cattle were now showing poor
The ground was almost bare and no fodder to be shared
This Country would be devastated if trade was to be no more
Whatever would they do if their land was not restored

It was time to work together and new tactics were in sight
So authorities in head office sent inspectors deep into the Outback
Reports came in thick and fast about the Farmer's current plight
It was obvious they needed help to get them back on track
People were in dire straits but they were prepared to fight
They only needed little help to set them up just right.

A New Beginning: NSW

POEMS

A New Beginning

They arrived a-plenty on huge ships from across the seas
With their only grubby clothing clinging to their backs
A land of promise they were told or so it seems
To toil for a mere pittance as so deemed or face the sack
But there was nowhere else to go when everything they lacked

With dirt under their fingernails and dust upon their clothes
They carved the earth to make it better for the host
Left behind were their families dying from fever in droves
Driven by ambition for a better life would rid them of their ghosts
Though they were the lucky ones or so they were often told

It was a 'New Beginning' everyone had said
A new Country too so strange but so far from home
Just work hard so tomorrow you will earn much more bread
Because if you don't you will find yourself cast out on your own
But they couldn't bear to say what was going through their heads

They carved themselves a future or so they thought it would be
Instead they laid foundations for brighter things ahead
However years of labor came no profits that they could see
It would be descendants they realized to reap rewards instead
'No matter…It is for our sons and daughters…We laid their beds.'

JENNY MAC

Gold Rush: VIC

Gold Rush

Wagons hit the dusty trails where bullock teams were driven
With picks and shovels and mere possessions they persevered
Though by solely on a promise of rewards were they living
Food was scarce and water too and so little money to be shared

A call had come to bear 'Gold Rush!' A land of riches to be had
So they had packed in haste to join the race
In their sights only promised gold that sent them all quite mad
Not knowing where to live amongst hordes of people in one space

They called it the diggings so now that would be their place
That is if they ever found the elusive gem they all called gold
It was mud and slush they lived in just to keep up with the pace
But determination urged them on by stories they were told

It could have been a disease that spread across the land
Infectious was its effect as others spread the word around
So newcomers faltered with no proper equipment at hand
But were clever enough to discover the true wealth to be found.

In Outback Country: SA

In Outback Country

It was land of sweeping plains of deserts cruel and harsh
Grasses shriveled up and died where the livestock fell like flies
Once where water flowed freely cracked river beds now a marsh
Waters ebbed to dissipate dried up creeks now boggy lies
'Rain! Rain!' they cried 'Before everything up and dies'

Sadly there was no answered prayers as then came more disaster
Huge fires roared across the fields homesteads reduced to naught
As the land was in remorse sweeping plains now charred pastures
Trees blackened from the wrath of dreaded fires after a drought

There was no reprieve for it to change but nature takes its course
Then the earth at once was drenched as rain pelted down instead
Rain in 'Outback Country' was scarce then came its dreadful force
Creeks cracked and dried now overfilled to be where yabbies bred
So too rivers overflowed their banks to create a massive flood

Then as in life's cycle land heals itself as grasses grew in clusters
Just when things were looking good there was wildlife galore
Livestock thrived and bred to more than they could muster
So much to contend with in this cruel harsh land of seasons four.

Deep in the Heart: WA

Deep in the Heart

It is a state of wonder of great magnitude in girth
If you want raw beauty then seek and you will find it all
Uniquely placed in a mighty desert 'Deep in the Heart' It's worth
As Floral Emblems forged from desert born plants will enthrall

Wildflowers and cactus bloom in many awkward ways
Though in a desert cruel and dry they spring up in odd places
Cracks in rocks and butts of trees anywhere their roots will stay
Little rainfall to keep them going just dirt dwelling dusty traces

Beneath the surface you may find a metal shining bright
Many have discovered just what it's like to make such a strike
Finding gold a massive nugget deep in the ground is quite a sight
They tell tales of sizes many ears at campfires have heard the like

Then strange enough amongst it all you could be mistaken
Though if you've travelled far inland you must visit now the coast
Pristine beaches on a coastline long will leave you quite shaken
So much beauty in one place so to take it all in is simply the most.

Paradise: QLD

Paradise

Australian beaches became famous around the world
Tourists were full of information as the word had got around
So they flocked to take advantage of all sights they would behold
Then spread stories of ventures down under to others they found

They called it 'Paradise' but only one of glory amongst the rest
Much to choose from only a single road out of the city to be found
People held up for hours flocked to beaches heedless of the test
Then stayed until they tanned their bodies on the sandy ground

Holidays were spent at beaches either with family or school camps
Where children from The Outback saw the ocean for the first time
They pitched their tents and had a dormitory come tent revamped
To all it was the highlight of their lives to remember down the line

Tourists and locals clambered into glass bottom boats in a row
To another haven Australia's 'Great Barrier Reef' a showcase itself
Where coral was viewed from boats and fish of all species on show
From the Ocean to the Tablelands they turned over every leaf.

Dreamtime: NT

Dreamtime

They called it 'Dreamtime' when they walked upon the land
Their presence firmly etched in caves upon the walls
So primitive their race spears and boomerangs in their hands
To hunt and fish just to survive they really had it all

It was a time of freedom but they battled against all odds
Guided just by stars as they ventured in the night
They found pure water holes camped by rivers when they could
Just to give back to the land a little was their only dream in sight

Their diet was a simple fare of berries or edible roots around
They lived on goanna's snakes even kangaroo and lizards
If they were lucky and their spear could bring them to the ground
Hunting was curbed by tools they made so they were not wizards
Just primitive folk who lived off the land without a future plan

Skills passed down from elders in the tribe was their only way
Their main existence was to survive but to protect the land
So they learnt about the land and bush to survive another day
Though always stayed within the tribe to contribute first hand

They moved to different places and for a short while would stay
An old habit was their 'Walkabout' is when they would roam
Across the land from waterhole to waterhole in a day
At night they ate their fill and danced because they were home.

JENNY MAC

The End of the World: TAS

The End of the World

It was of Australia's History as the old stories had been told
Of scenes not so pretty just brutality there instead
Notorious penal colonies for convict prisoners they would hold
Who lived their life in hardship and starving without bread

Across the seas they called it 'The End of the World' down under
A place from prying eyes where in droves convicts were sent
On ships to a place called Van Diemen's Land to set them asunder
To be imprisoned for their wrongs is where their life was spent

Prison life was harsh beyond belief on most it left a mark
Where doomed escapes were the norm for any prison break
As they drowned or starved there was no relief or take
Only if unlucky instead of floggings they were eaten by the sharks

Most attempted an escape that was to their regret
Guards finding them out made display of them with a penalty fee
So much more than they could cope with or to extremes met
Their bodies spent mere flesh and bone was all left to see
To live in hardship and filth no food would dictate their death.

JENNY MAC

Native Flowers of Australia

Australian Wildflowers

Unique to Australia the pretty wildflowers and native's bloom
Along the Coastline in the Outback and the Desert too
Each season sharing a special array a treat as each petal looms
To distinguish Australia uniquely amongst the very few

Every nook and cranny and amongst rock formations too
Even in the desert was where our 'Australian Wildflowers' grew
Pride is our Floral protégé's and Floral Emblems to name a few
Our National heritage not something learnt is what we just knew.

Australia

Remote Australia

Communication was a problem with the outside world way back
No television mobiles or computers a wireless an only link for that
Roads were bare dirt and muddy in the wet and just barely a track
So travel took many hours with chained tyres or there you sat

Road trains were first to venture out for deliveries or moving stock
Until train tracks snaked overland a puffing billy to pride of place
Movie theaters showing stars from other countries was a shock
As they were myths so unreachable to Australians not in the race

It was deep in the Outback where brave tourists dared to tread
Survival was an Australians way of life in floods fire and drought
So visitors found Australian wildlife threatening all hopes instead
As for Australians with local knowledge were yet to lose a bout.

Then slowly but surely just like the sun would rise each day
Australia was changing so the world finally took notice at last
Wild Outback Country and best beaches visitors were told about
A modern Australia to explore not a 'Remote Australia' of the past

Endless plains sweep Outback Australia the oceans green or blue
As seasons change a haven materializes after a dreaded drought
Mountain ranges to sandy beaches and the Outback beckons you
From the Ocean to the Outback much beauty to witness no doubt.

JENNY MAC

Wishes in the Wind: ACT

Australian Capital
Territory

Wishes in the Wind

Though help came in moderation it was not nearly enough
To combat the dreaded seasons in The Australian Outback
Properties suffered severely and made living there quite tough
They needed more assistance to keep them fighting back

Pleas were sent from near and far right across the land
Words heard of their situation were just 'Wishes in the Wind'
No-one really knew of their plight they had all wiped their hands
Thinking the job was done but had no more funds to find

It was then the properties faltered with no prospects in sight
People forced to sell what little stock remained
Just to stay alive and stay afloat for one more night
Or they were faced with failure their pride was now their pain

Some lasted longer than others forcing themselves to stay
Though eventually life's cruelty prevented them from gaining
Their once rich property couldn't be given away
So people walked off their land their hearts and souls remaining.

Beginning a Life: NSW

POEMS

Beginning a Life

Some people worked in shipyards and all along the dock
Though others ventured further out into the Country to find
Where a few stations were found to be raising stock
So they toiled as station hands which was alien to their mind

Weeks turned to months and then years went by
They really had no option but to keep working hard to survive
Though little did they know that they were not living just a lie
Because it seems they were setting up a future that would thrive

Some saved their earnings and this gave them a start
Though to own a piece of land in Australia was unheard of
But with determination they persisted and looked upon a chart
Of drawings of their home in a land they had come to love

So now the progress started and dwellings were sprouting out
Australians now they were making their place amongst the old
Where Australians shared what they had to make it come about
Then they all lived side by side or as the stories were told about

In Australia 'Beginning a Life' with others shouting out a pact
This is our land our home now for everyone to see for a fact
It had come from hard work from The Ocean to The Outback
So across the land they conquered with their prides still intact.

A New type of Gold: VIC

A New type of Gold

Long hard days of digging in the earth
How would they make their fortune if no gold was to be found
Just to be rewarded or compensated for spending all their worth
Soon they discovered 'A New type of Gold' not in the ground

It came to their attention as they hacked around in slush too long
For everyone they visited had an urgent plea of what was lacked
It was widely broadcasted as they moved amongst the throng
Their cries being music to their ears as they then hurriedly packed

There was very little water in a creek they shared just up a pace
Though the main cry for help was for food that would not go sour
They knew now what to do to get rich in this here place
It wasn't gold they sort…Real riches were to be had from flour

That is how it started from the diggings to the city and back
Their bullock teams were loaded with sacks and sacks of flour
So the business grew like wildfire catering for all needs in tact
'No-one else thought of doing it so all profits scored are ours.'

Doomed in Outback Country SA

It was in an Australian Desert one man learnt first-hand
His life was 'Doomed in Outback Country' a lesson to be learnt
To dig for gold as he was told was little to his gain
He packed his gear disheartened and disgruntled without a find
Endless digging the dirt his energy spent but so too was his mind

His heart beat faster as he checked his water bag only then to find
That it left but just a trickle
Oh Me! Oh My! To believe yarns of wealth to be had from others
He had listened 'How could I be so fickle?'
Still way out there The Outback Desert seemed to beckon
He felt alone deep in a desert that was brutal to be said
Then to top it all severe heat set in to threaten
Though that wasn't all his woes as he trudged along in dread
When from lack of water his horse just fell down dead

With mouth so dry and swollen he combed the shriveled Country
Where mirages danced odd shapes appeared of promised water
Then to find it was just a respite from mother earth's cruel bounty
As it failed him miserably for certain when it didn't prove to cater

His pain was a living thing now so out loud he prayed
He yelled of his grief as he tottered and swayed about to fall
'How could this land do this to me … It is my home … After all.'

Continued:
Doomed in Outback Country

Then dark clouds blanketed the sky, he found it hard to see
He blinked and looked upwards as the heavens opened out
So with rising fist he raged and shouted out his thanks with glee
Rain fell thunder clapped so loudly his senses shook about

He danced in thanks and dived in it and drank his muddy fill
Then lightning struck right beside him to suck up all his mirth
As it struck all around him he stood so very still
Left to wonder would he survive this latest bout on Mother Earth

He looked at the land around him which could have claimed his
life as small rivulets formed now and relief was just in sight
His vision blurred he could barely see as figures formed ahead
Were they mirages or finally someone to tell them of his plight

Though sadly he also knew for a fact…If he lived to tell his tale…
They would just stare at him… Shake their heads… and wonder…
'What all the fuss was about?'

Beauty at the Heart WA

Beauty at the Heart

Though it was not only minerals of beauty to be found
As miners discovered and tourists noted 'Beauty at the Heart'
Way up north where mountains formed were gorges to astound
Coloured rocks of ochre displayed a brilliance for just a start

Secret caves and hide-a-ways enhanced the visitor's thrills
Rock caverns housed some pristine rocks of value to be sure
It was a miner's paradise up in the ranges so the word was spilled
So many companies set up camp on a mighty scale ashore

For tourists though so much to see with wildlife everywhere
With cameras ready they were enthralled with all finds sublime
Beauty was all around them as flowers spouted almost anywhere
But to come face to face with a Kangaroo for tourists a special time

Unveiling true beauty is difficult at best so they combed the cliffs
To their surprise discovered where true nature was at its best
Water tumbled off the cliffs above the waterfall truly not a myth
It thundered splashing down to a crystal pool purer than the rest.

Country Paradise QLD

Country Paradise

From the Ocean to The Outback they sought out this land
Proud country farmers found the soil so rich for growing crops
Across the mountains into a mecca for each and every hand
Farming was to be a way of life the produce would be tops

Not only crops were Australia's worth as paddocks were stocked
The Country prospered and rode to victory on the sheep's back
Merino sheep that is…famous for their wool… not to be mocked
For sheep put Australia on the map its trade was right on track

Other stock of fame was to be the Angus and Hereford Cattle
They bred true Aussie stock that lasted through the ages
In early days though getting them to sale-yards was a battle
Roads were tough in the wet as they crammed the trucks cages

Dairy farms were built especially for their stars
Their distinctive black and white a special trade-mark to boast
Friesian cattle were milked to produce the best milk by far
Australia thrived in 'Country Paradise' Aussie stock match a host.

Land of Dreams NT

Land of Dreams

It was while living in a 'Land of Dreams' their stories were told
Passed down through the ages for new blood coming up to strive
Around the campfires they sat each recalling their tales so bold
   It was the only way they knew to keep their dreams alive

   They had no claim on where they lived so yarns were spun
   In later years it was recalled that they may have been the first
   To wander through the bush seeking necessities was no shun
But a way of survival to seek out food and water for their thirst

   Their way of life was primitive no treasures to be had or sort
   Instead they stayed in close relationship with mother earth
So making weapons to aid them in a hunt was what they thought
Would be reward to feed the tribes and should prove their worth

So in the dusk men grabbed their spears the women made the fires
   Into the scrub they went and hunted for dinner to feed the clan
   Young girls dug for grubs and picked wild berries to stay alive
While in the creeks young boys fished or dug up what they could

   It was a celebration each and every night something to foretell
   They sang and danced to give thanks to what food was offered
     A corrobboree was the tribal dance they all knew so well
Something they had all learnt from the elders who had proffered.

The Isle of Plenty: TAS

The Isle of Plenty

Life was tough for prisoners many sent underground to fold
Many starved and now through Historic Sites the stories were told
As reminders of a punishing past now history in museums of old
As tours of grounds and buildings was where the truths unfold

So on these scenic sites where cruelty was often shed
Convicts rarely sited tranquil waters they dug up ground instead
In penance for their only crime of stealing a loaf of bread
Labouring underground no land in sight so deep in dirt they tread

It was a land for brutality no other reason to be found
Only convicts paid a price for wrong doings they did commit
But then decades later as word had got around
There were other ways of treating them as the latest conflict hit

Convicts had been severely treated but then came a new trend
For logging in forests for building ships and furniture making
It was the convicts they would send
So at last they got a decent meal for the jobs they were undertaking

Of those survivor's reward was found in paid wages for toil
Going into a new era a chance or mere hope for a better life
So ancestors paved a way for descendants in 'The Isle of Plenty'
To live a life enjoy their lot that to them had cost lots of strife.

JENNY MAC

True Blue

True Blue

It could have been A Jolly Swagman or a Banker in the Grand
A Ringer in the long yard a Stockman or Drover to name a few
Either in the City or The Outback deep in Bush across the land
They were all Aussies to be sure who earnt the brand 'True Blue'

It wasn't taken lightly by those who earnt this tag
It was of stories told about them by others close at hand
Where some were there to question they weren't about to brag
But rather accepted it as an honour and proof of this their land

It was Australia after all their pride as countrymen complete
Just to be given the nick-name 'True Blue'
Was to them the biggest treat
To be looked upon as legends stand-outs through and through
So stories carried these legends from the Ocean to the Outback
Though it took many years or decades the mighty legends grew
Just to be an Australian was good enough and no proof was lacked
If Aussie pride runs deep inside you knew you were 'True Blue.'

JENNY MAC

Australia

Australia Down Under

When technology took over old habits were truly lost
As time had passed what worked once was just not good enough
To compete against the world Australia changed for the host
A simple life forever gone so for older Australian's life was rough

To become a number instead of a name was a shame to behold
People found just to welcome change a most difficult cross to bear
Though Australians made of sturdy stock had listened to tales told
So bucked in to do their bit survival won by new trades and wares

Cities prospered the Outback grew in 'Australia Down Under'
As the world looked on in wonder of this far-away land
That not many knew of but now no man could put asunder
Because Aussie spirit was just one thing Australians had in hand

New land was sort in cities as towns sprouted in the bush
Population overtook progress a rush for prime land was a must
To claim a plot along the ocean-front there was a mighty push
Though it became the wealthy who reaped rewards for their lust

Modern cities grew the County thrived new suburbs spread afar
So progress to cater for the multitude was stepped up to cope
Railway lines snaked across the earth and roads now made of tar
Looking back how it all began it was a shock to compare the scope.

Respite was on the Wind: ACT

Australian Capital
Territory

Respite was on the Wind

As time went by and seasons changed so too did the land
Where once the paddocks were withered dry and bare
Now it flourished as new grasses grew amongst very little sand
As the earth was rich once more in even places it would rarely fare

Go to The Outback they cried the land is ripe for the picking
So land was bought cheaper than their predecessors had in size
Who for their life's work got but just a licking
As new farmers reaped rewards from their unfortunate demise

It was fortunate for those who didn't have to battle all their lives
They were the lucky ones who just happened along behind
To prosper in a land of plenty now they surely would survive
Make a living in The Outback when 'Respite was on the Wind'

Sad but true this land is harsh and Aussies find it tough
But it restored the farmer's faith to continue in their quest
To succeed in this great Outback would be just reward enough
It was their life's dream so they know they did their very best.

Beginning Again: NSW

Beginning Again

Though many were saddened by the loss of loved ones declined
This land was their home now they had earnt it over time
To begin again and start everything afresh was their only bind
In memory of their families that they had to leave behind

Australia had become home now so they learnt of Aussie pride
It was something not given but something earnt in a long while
If they had remained then they too would surely have died
So to live in a new Country with new friends they learnt to smile

Their past was soon a memory as they set down their roots
Who would have thought that at the start they would succeed
It was determination to survive which gave them all a boost
To better things a place called home where they could breed

It was for sons and daughters that they toiled to make it suffice
An endless task they would document down for them to peruse
At a later date as they left this earth this land they had made nice
Reward would go to their children who would have plenty to use

As in their future they would add to what they had gained
So working hard to build a life
Was just as simple as 'Beginning Again.'
If their parents did it so too would they sacrifice to bear the strife.

For the Taking: VIC

For the Taking

So it was the mighty gold rush that they all had heard about
But their fortune wasn't gold at all and they were not mistaking
It was hard work and lots of hours before they could shout
Real wealth is providing food it was just there 'For the Taking'

So when in the city it was the high life that they led
A thriving business in buying flour for just a few measly bob
Then selling it at the diggings where big profits were to be had
It was their life now not digging for gold but a new-found job

They would soldier on until they had banked enough savings
Which in their minds would buy a farm for what they wished for
A place to call home and a living to be made was their craving
To raise some sheep and grow crop so they would not be poor

After all it is why they came here all they needed was the drive
To work hard and earn a life but fate took them to the diggings
So luck was all it took for them to survive
They didn't need to be on a ship no more way up in the riggings.

JENNY MAC

Seeking the Outback: SA

Seeking the Outback

Though many stories had been told The Outback kept a bidding
'Seeking the Outback' Come find wonders the whispers softly say
Should we venture out the tourists asked or else it will be hidden
So who knows what we'll find, forget stories told, we go today

From the safety of the pristine coast they ventured inland a piece
They wanted adventure at least something chic to brag about
So they spurned threats of danger until it put them in a niche
Now their distress was evident in their fight to get back out

But where to go no one was sure and their water getting low
We just go back the way we came someone softly said
They looked across the landscape bare so nothing there to show
If we don't get out of here they will find we'll all be dead

So just as spirits were dissipated and no input of their plight
We should have listened to the others they agreed and said
As they looked to the horizon and cheered as help was in sight
Or was it a mirage that cruelly gave them hope instead.

Digging Deep: WA

Digging Deep

A land of opportunity of riches in the earth
They dug with huge machinery open cut mines deep in the dirt
Money was the drawcard for anyone with skills or worth
So they mined for minerals to earn the living they had learnt

'Digging Deep' in the land they searched it for its wealth
Trade was imperative and they knew the goods were there
But so too Australian locals needed work to maintain their health
So workers a-plenty came from near and far to earn their share

Mining companies ruled and spread their wings across the land
It did not matter to them at all where they went
They set up camp in areas either remote or close at hand
After all when done and dusted it was a Country to be their vent

However many a one prospered from this vent upon their home
Loads of work was offered and big money to be had
They called it prosperity so no-one disagreed or groaned
They got on with the task ahead and forgot all about the dread.

Treasures in Paradise: QLD

Treasures in Paradise

Much to do and see but 'Treasures in Paradise' varieties are found
Resources so many like sugar-cane and wheat silos to name a few
Though coal is dug up from the earth used to power all surrounds
Solar Power gained from Australian sun was creeping up like new

   Cities link the Outback with transport and locomotives too
Tarred roads made driving pleasure now to how it was back a way
Travel in Australia by road rail or air will surely be to please you
Once home to continue a way of life when a break made your day

Then in the north if its sport you seek or adventure to be found
Fishermen test their strength against Marlin on a line was the most
   Massive fish that fight like nothing else upon the ground
   To land a Marlin is a mighty feat true fishermen would boast

   Though we have talked about resources and beauty a bounty
  The real treasures in this land of ours may be pretty or adverse
It is people who give Australia a lift true Aussies of the Country
  Without their pride and dedication things could be a lot worse.

JENNY MAC

Daytime Dreaming: NT

Daytime Dreaming

Australia was changing and so too was the land
So 'Daytime dreaming' become a way of life for most
Who wanted all the benefits of living in a new world at hand
Many sort out jobs as station hands some ventured to the coast

Others joined a community not to just live out in the bush
They got hired and earnt money and could buy what they needed
So things were looking up and to the eager ones it became a rush
As they were competing now as their passions were heeded

Some made it into Parliament others chose a different route
The world called for more talent to be had and raised the bar
So to stand in front of a cheering crowd was to be their bout
To prove to the world they were good enough by far

Many great competitors too have made this Country proud
Olympic gold around their necks as they graced the dais first
Great achievements great rewards earnt by hard work to astound
A path of glory was where they trod to be the world's best

Then there were the talented ones of the movie-world ilk
Acting became a pathway to greater things of late
To mix it with the legends seemed apart like cotton and silk
But to raise the crowds to new levels was how they all would rate.

The Apple Isle: TAS

The Apple Isle

Explorers found this place they called 'The Apple Isle'
An extension of Australia's culture but separated too
So beautiful the land so they settled there in style
Blood, sweat and tears were spent. They toiled to see it through

Now they named it Tasmania when the settlers arrived
They were from all walks of life but now called it their home
It was through hard work that they all had strived
To make a place livable so no more would they roam

So much history about the past was obvious to most
Just strolling through the streets they saw buildings of old
Where prisoners held within the walls now dictated to the host
To read of their misfortune long ago in the past were stories told

Now tourists visit to learn a culture that was sacred in the past
Many people learnt of what made Tasmania what it is
Where the locals came from was revealed at last
As descendants of a mix of migrants who ventured to this bliss

So through cobblestone streets they wander in awe of many traits
Down on the dock's ships waited to take them aboard
As people were commuting to Australia just across the strait
On a ship they called 'The Princess' of Tasmania they stood proud.

Wallaroo and Joey

Red Kangaroo

Grey Kangaroo and Joey

POEMS

Australian Animals in the Wild

Koala Bear

Wildlife survive harsh conditions in the land that they were bred
So unique to Australia their livelihood our heritage forever more
Of many species there are others of goannas and snakes to be said
As huge crocodiles roam on land and in water predators for sure

Across open fields and clay-pans Big Red Kangaroo's dwell
In mulga or scrubby areas are Greys and old man Walla Roo's too
Australian icons Kangaroo and Emu to breast our emblem is a sell
Only safe to roam Wombats or Porcupines species to name a few

In gum trees high Koala's feed on eucalyptus leaves in content
In shallow creeks a Platypus hides from prying eyes on the shore
Such variety is our wildlife to list them all would be an advent
To say the least multitudes of creatures live amongst us with lore

Platypus

Many dangerous snakes slither in long grasses
In hollow logs you may find a King Brown
Aptly known to be the deadliest of them all
Though others can be fatal to the masses

While high in the treetops
No nest is safe from giant goannas after eggs
They scale up trees great claws gripping bark
In their quest to just get fed they don't renege
No birds can compete so they fly off with a squawk.   *Wombat*

Australia

Modern Australia

Surprisingly the bustle in cities can be just as wild as in the bush
Traffic noise from highways twisting like an octopus has it in grips
All reflections that came along when technology gave its push
Australia is raw but modern with endless rewarding bits.

Yes this became 'Modern Australia' to compete against the world
Technology available across the board to all the Country's States
Australian movies where screened legends born to lay a new mold
Athletes shined competing for gold in the Olympics was their fate
Proudly singing the Australian Anthem 'Advance Australia Fair'

World travel was as easy now as flying inter-state
So Australians ventured from their comforts to visit countries afar
Whereas a long time past no such luxury could they contemplate
Australia was far behind as a younger land but now were on a par

Tourists flocked to pristine beaches in cities they saw the lights
They spent their Aussie holidays in what we have for life
Much interest was in resources available to all they had in sight
To spend idle hours and money for pleasures had with no strife

So it is Australia they all come to seek out adventure to be found
Once a laid-back Country now a busy hub for visitors to comb
To visit a famous Outback each nook and cranny or camp- ground
But Australians all rejoice to call this land Australia… 'Home.'

This is Australiana ... 'Ocean to the Outback'

National Emblem

Red Kangaroo

Emu

Eagle

Australia
Australian Floral Emblems

Saltwater Crocodile

Goanna

POEMS

Australiana
'POEMS'
'Ocean to the Outback'

'From the Ocean'

Seagull

Australian Seascape

Wedge-Tailed Eagle

Crow

'To the Outback'

Australian Outback Landscape

Australiana

Australian Floral Emblems

www.ingramcontent.com/pod-product-compliance
Lightning Source LLC
Chambersburg PA
CBHW051540010526
44107CB00064B/2797